Spark Plug

An Endearing Dog Story

Happy Reading!
Loads of Love!
Sheri Palmer

Sheri Palmer

Copyright © 2023 Sheri Palmer
All rights reserved
First Edition

Fulton Books
Meadville, PA

Published by Fulton Books 2023

All rights are reserved. This book is protected by the copyright laws of the United States of America. No part of this book may be stored electronically, transmitted, copied, reproduced, or reprinted for commercial gain or profit without prior written permission from Sheri Palmer.

ISBN 979-8-88731-752-6 (paperback)
ISBN 979-8-88731-764-9 (hardcover)
ISBN 979-8-88731-753-3 (digital)

Printed in the United States of America

This book is dedicated to all people of the world, professional or not, who have passionately dedicated their lives, time, and finances to rescue, protect, heal, educate, and care for humanity and animals of all kinds who need a helping hand.

Thank you!

Without them, underdogs could never reach their full potentials of becoming super dogs!

Chapter 1

By the heated conversation, I could tell my Grandfather wanted no part of this Rottweiler puppy. The man who accidentally hit and killed our dog the day before returned with a tiny puppy in his arms for a replacement. Grandfather, under the impression it was dangerous, refused to accept the baby Rottweiler being gifted to him. The man explained what great farm dogs and family pets they make. Since he was a top breeder of purebred Rottweilers, my grandfather listened to him. He explained that this batch of puppies was solely bred for his own personal stock of breeders and not for sale. They were sired by the most intelligent, even-tempered, purebred registered dogs he owned, and this puppy showed the highest in quality possible, the greatest of all the dogs he'd ever had. The men put the puppy down, walking away from the fenced front yard, out of ears' reach of us as the conversation intensified. Voices rising and under duress of just losing a special herding and guard dog did not make this exchange comfortable for either man. We'd just lost our beautiful white collie, which had been trained extra well for all expected of him on a farm. Most farmers needed herding dogs and a guard dog and loving pet. We had been blessed having one dog for both—a rarity. Everyone was heartbroken for the loss. I was taking it the hardest, losing my first friend and constant companion, playmate, and babysitter. He had been the greatest pillow I'd ever owned.

Our attention focused back on this tiny black ball with golden brown boots and a golden-brown star on his chest, chasing a grass snake. My brother and I questioned if he was a police dog or a sheriff with a built-in badge displayed on his chest. His tail was straight up in the air, circling around as fast as a helicopter propeller. He was not like other dogs that wag their tails side to side and hang downwardly.

He was an unusual dog, and I was entertained watching all his quirky moves, but my judging ability needed improving since I was four years old, and there was only one dog to compare him to. He was funny, and he was tremendously happy to be here on our farm. Acting like he was plugged into an electrical wall socket, he was overly energized, and obviously, he loved it here. He did not seem to mind that he was abruptly taken away from his mother dog and puppy siblings. I wondered if the little creature knew it was his job to be our pet before he even got here, with the way he displayed his approval. He seemed satisfied with his life journey already being decided for him.

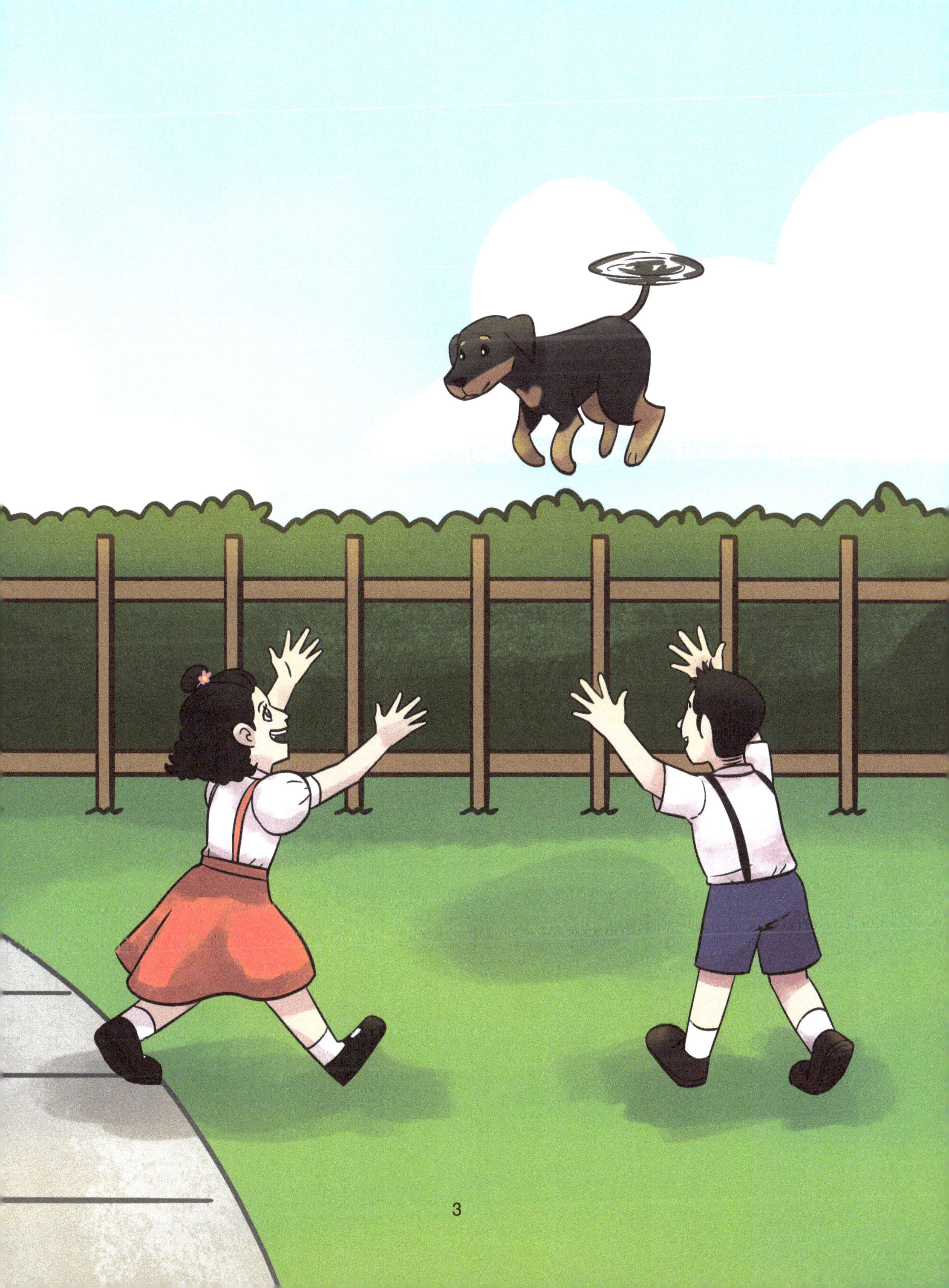

Grandfather decided to give him a chance for two weeks. We were happy with that for now. The breeder shook Grandfather's hand, claiming he would never regret the decision to try him and left on good terms. We took the energy-filled wiggle worm into the house and made him a bed behind the potbellied stove in the kitchen by laying an oversized quilt down after feeding him and cuddling with him. He then started yawning, and we put him on the floor. He retreated to his bed and started digging and biting his quilt, pawing repeatedly to a make a perfect bed to sleep on. He piled the huge quilt up high like a giant ice cream cone. Jumping up, he made it to the top, lay down with a sigh, and yawned, laying his head between his front paws. A minute later, he put one paw over his nose, reminding me of a human baby sucking their thumbs. His constant tail spinning slowly stopped as he slept for the first time, hopefully in his new lifetime home. My brother and I wanted him desperately.

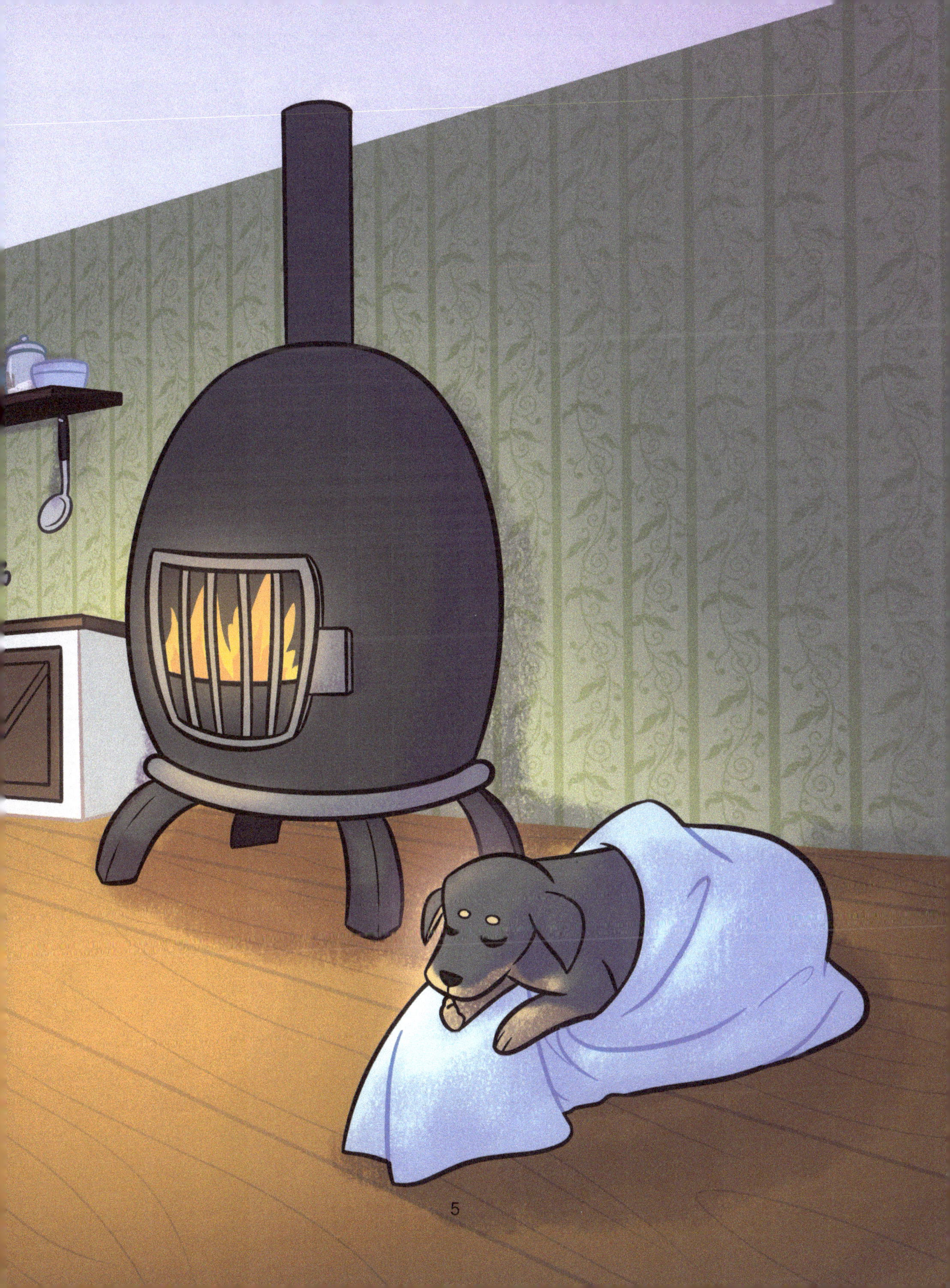

Bark, bark, bark! Someone woke up early. He was running fast in the air, lying across Grandfather's forearm to journey outdoors. After business was taken care of in the grass, he bounced back to the house for breakfast, ready for a big day of exploring his farm.

His tail spun straight up over his back, and he was always full of energy. The family watched, noticing he almost glowed of electricity, happily rolling around, running, and jumping. We named him Spark Plug. He even sparked us into happiness just by watching him.

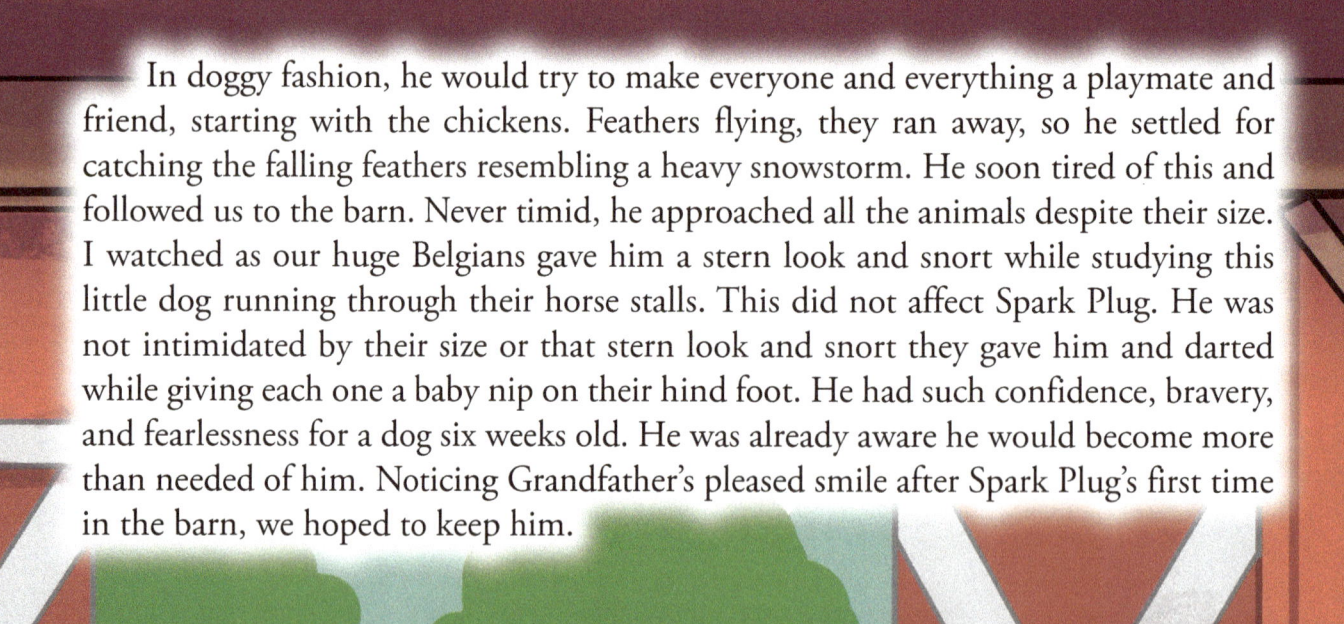

In doggy fashion, he would try to make everyone and everything a playmate and friend, starting with the chickens. Feathers flying, they ran away, so he settled for catching the falling feathers resembling a heavy snowstorm. He soon tired of this and followed us to the barn. Never timid, he approached all the animals despite their size. I watched as our huge Belgians gave him a stern look and snort while studying this little dog running through their horse stalls. This did not affect Spark Plug. He was not intimidated by their size or that stern look and snort they gave him and darted while giving each one a baby nip on their hind foot. He had such confidence, bravery, and fearlessness for a dog six weeks old. He was already aware he would become more than needed of him. Noticing Grandfather's pleased smile after Spark Plug's first time in the barn, we hoped to keep him.

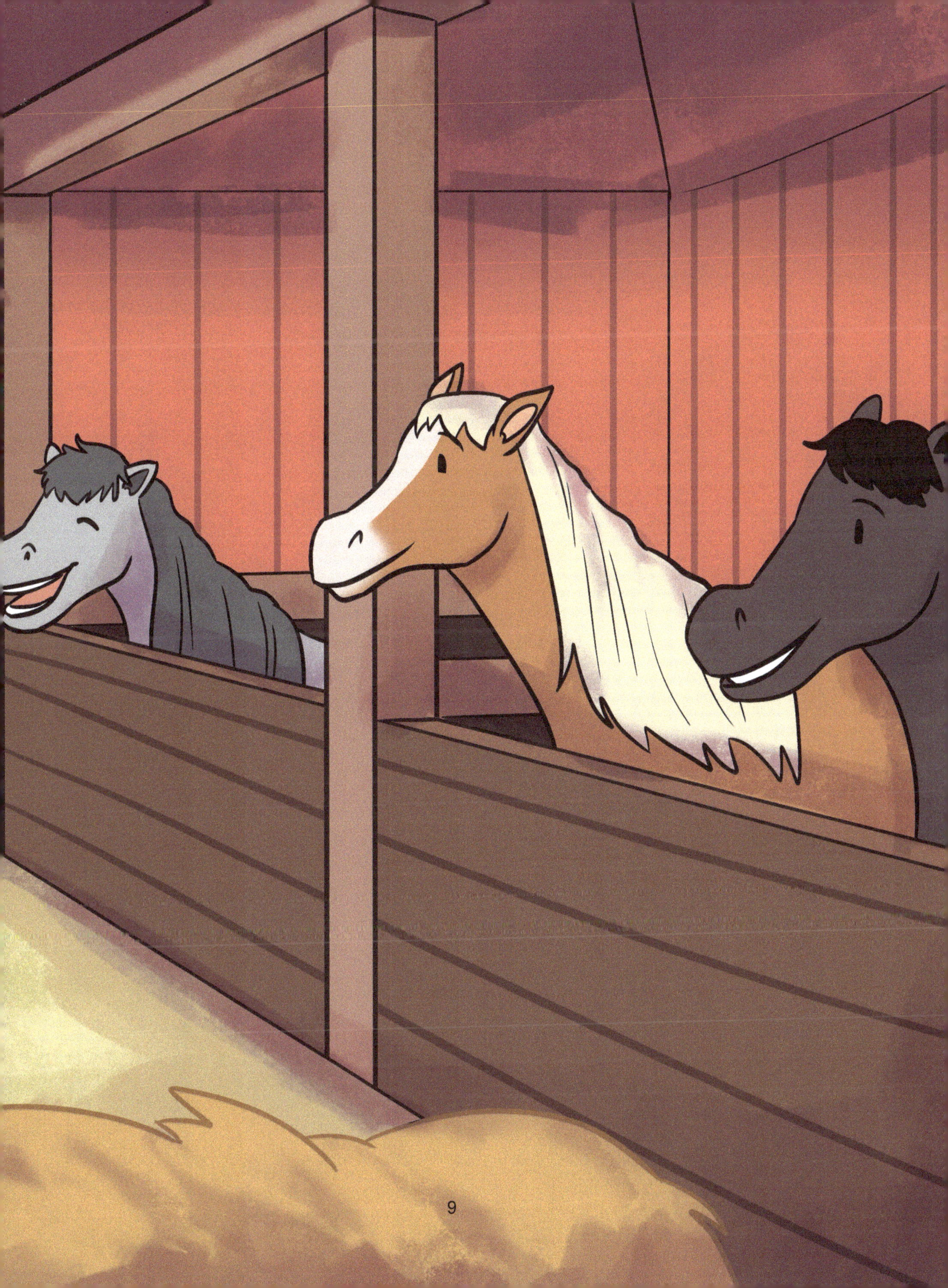

Chapter 2

    Realizing the puppy was not in view and hoping he was napping, us kids went to find him. He was content, lying on his stomach in the backyard, mouth closed and paws over his nose, trying to hide something. We approached, and he gave a baby growl while spinning his helicopter propeller tail, reassuring us that he did not want to share or part with his newly found treasure. We would need Grandfather for this, knowing a growling animal is not safe to approach.

Grandfather snatched him up. Hearing a muffled chirping sound coming from inside his mouth, he opened the baby dog's mouth, and out jumped a cricket. We all laughed, even Spark Plug, with a very satisfied happy-face expression. It was hard to tell how long the cricket had to endure being a hostage, but it was unharmed and jumped away safely.

During milking, he went with us kids to gather the herd of cows and bring them from the pasture into the barn to be milked. He loved this even though he would get in front of them and bark, causing them to turn back to the pasture. Not long after, he understood the routine of cows—go in to get milked then out to pasture. During milking, he lay on his bed by the calf pen, on his quilt on top of straw for comfort. He enjoyed watching all the cats who came during milking for a drink of milk. This is where Spark Plug had to be chained up to wait for his turn at the milk dish. The dish was a huge iron skillet filled with warm milk, big enough to feed eighteen cats that helped keep the rodents from overtaking the feed that was stored for the cows and horses. Morning and night this was routine. If the cats drank it all, Grandfather made sure to pour more milk for the puppy. Life was delicious for Spark Plug—he'd find the calf pen and lick up all their droppings too. It looked like yellow pudding lying on the floor. I imagine it tasted like baby formula since that is all they ate.

When he gets older, he will sleep in the barn at night, guarding it from night thieves trying to steal milk, feed, and hay, along with medicine, tools, saddles, and livestock, especially calves. All is at risk from thieves. I was glad Spark Plug was with us.

When chores were done in the evening, Spark Plug ran like a marathon racer to the house. He knew he would be given a special bite of beef jerky, sometimes Grandfather's popcorn, or share Grandfather's onion and mustard sandwich with a sprinkle of salt, most coveted by both. After bedtime, the puppy automatically took his spot behind the stove. Occasionally, one of the house cats curled up with him. Everyone loved Spark Plug. He was such an unusual dog, and he intuitively realized he was part of a welcoming, loving family.

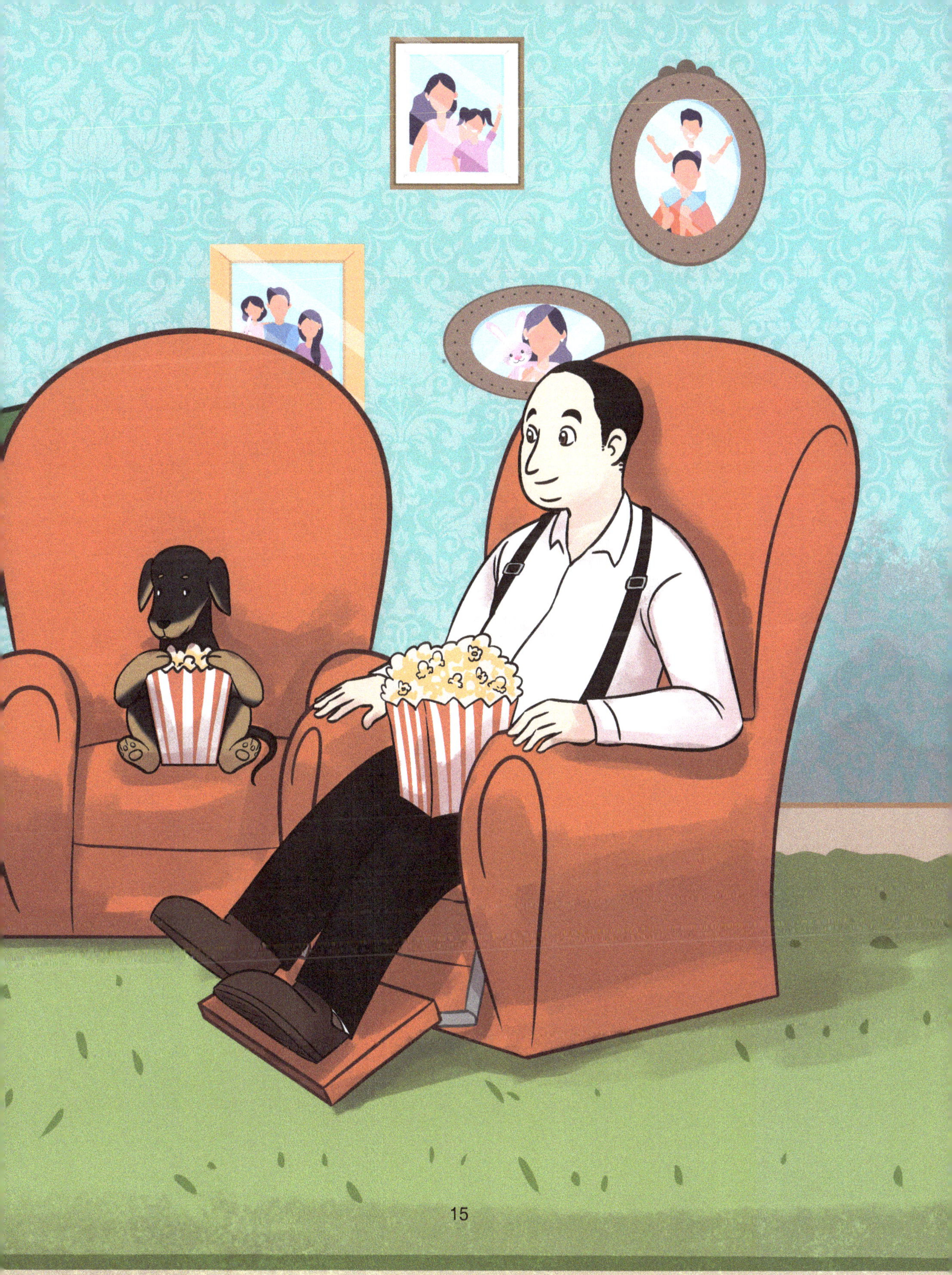

Every day the routine repeated, and time was passing fast. Spark Plug was now following the fence bordering the whole farm, three hundred and twenty acres of hills, swamp, thick woods, pastures, and orchard, along with two huge ponds after chores every morning. On occasion he would bring back a woodchuck, a living woodchuck, carrying it by the scruff of the neck. He liked bringing Grandmother living gifts, plus he got to play with them. He would bring them to the front door and lay them down. Then he would scratch and bark once while sitting patiently, guarding his offering until she opened the door, spinning his tail with his happy face on, happy to give gifts and happy he had a new animal friend. He loved to please his people.

Grandmother knew what was up when he came to the front door, blaming herself while praising the puppy so much when he found three kittens abandoned because of the death of their mother cat. Trying to birth more kittens caused him to keep bringing her baby animals to raise. Spark Plug did not move them; instead he ran and notified Grandmother in doggy fashion with a squeaky, excited, yet serious bark, coaxing her to follow him to the bush under the pantry window of the house. She brought them in the house, laid them in a box on a baby blanket, and gave them warmed milk while finding an eyedropper. She fed them one at a time and put them back in the box.

Spark Plug smelled the milk on their fur and began licking each one. He licked them clean and attended every feeding time, giving them a bath. They grew fast and followed him around, treating him like their mother. The three kittens and a big Rottweiler, all of them like they were from comic books, made us laugh at all the shenanigans they played and at seeing all three kittens asleep on top of him at night while he lay on his bed behind the potbellied stove. We'd strategically placed his bed there at first, knowing he would eventually be a guard dog, and it was at the center of the kitchen where the backdoor adjacent from the front door was. If anyone broke in, Spark Plug could see both doors while he lay hidden behind the stove. Around midnight, he would be taken to the barn and run loose 'til chore time at 4:00 am, when most thefts happened.

When Grandmother started chaining him up on a leash to go to the barn, amazingly, the training our docile, happy-face, tail-spinning dog received did not turn him into a vicious guard dog. The second she clicked the leash to his collar, he would lick her face then start snarling and drooling, growling the whole way to the barn, dragging Grandmother down the path with him. It amazes me even now how he instinctively knew what to do. There was never any break-ins.

Chapter 3

It was Spark Plug's birthday again, and as tradition, Grandmother made him a peanut butter cake with peanut butter icing and beef jerky sprinkles shaped like a dog's paw print on top. When they finished milking and all chores were finished, they headed to the house. Reaching the milkhouse exit door, Spark Plug jumped in front of them, whining while he jumped up, putting his paws on Grandfather's shoulders, preventing him from opening the door.

The full-grown 197-pound Rottweiler was serious. No tail spinning, no happy face, only verbally, in doggy fashion, trying to explain his crazy actions. We thought he wanted more milk. Grandfather tied him up so we could freely leave. Opening the door, he slammed it shut. We could hear the roaring, scratching, and vicious growling outside the door from a vicious black bear and hoped it would not get in.

Shortly it stopped, and we saw it heading for the river out the window. Seeing the bear leaving was a relief. It was safe again, and we all went to the house together but not until Grandfather hugged and vigorously petted Spark Plug, promising he would never doubt his guarding actions again. Instead of waiting for his birthday cake later, Grandfather went to the smokehouse and got him a big ham soup bone as a special thank-you for being a genuinely loving pet. It was a sight to see this 197-pound bodybuilder-looking Rottweiler do a wiggle-worm happy dance then roll on the ground with his bone in his mouth.

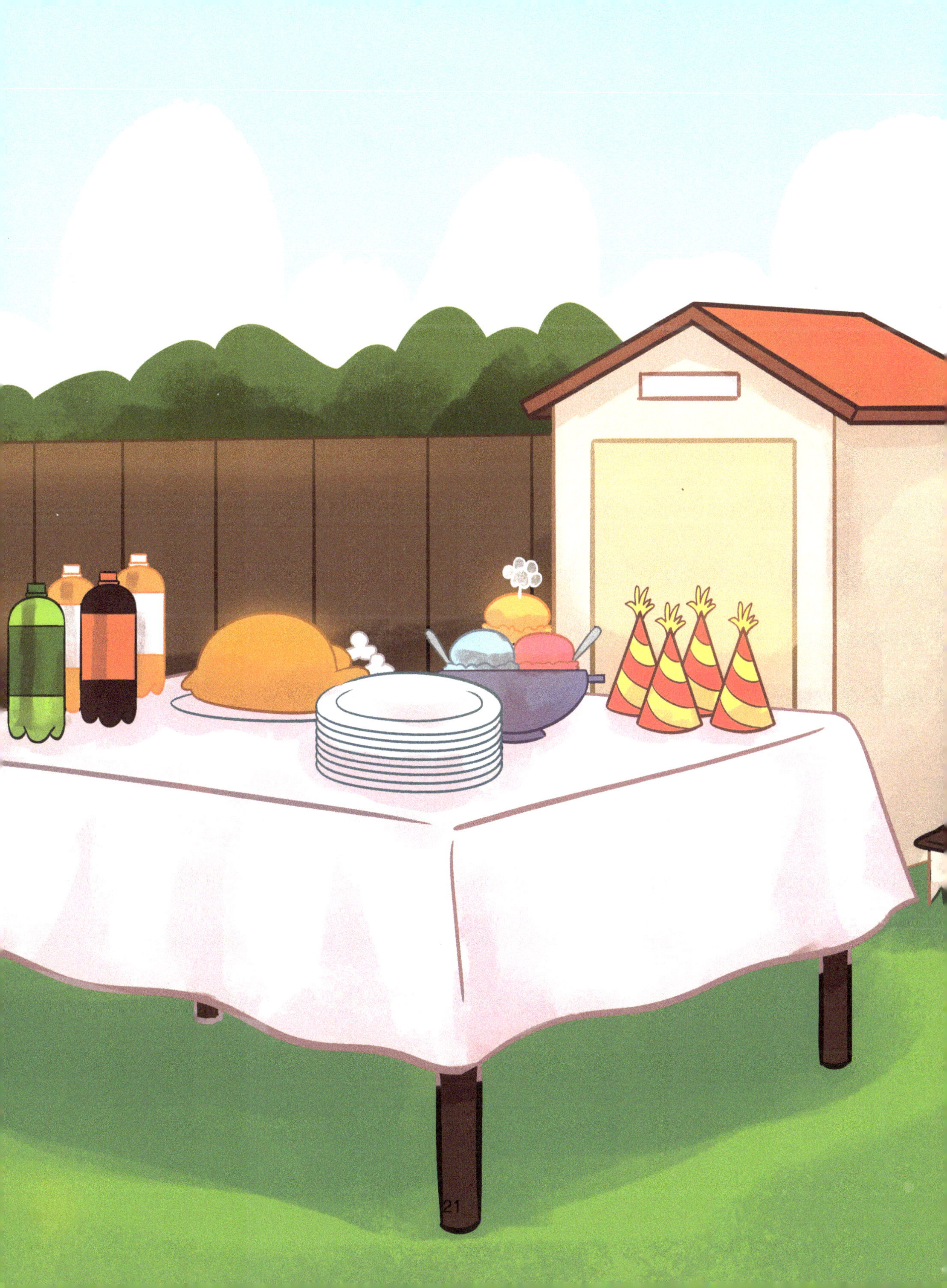

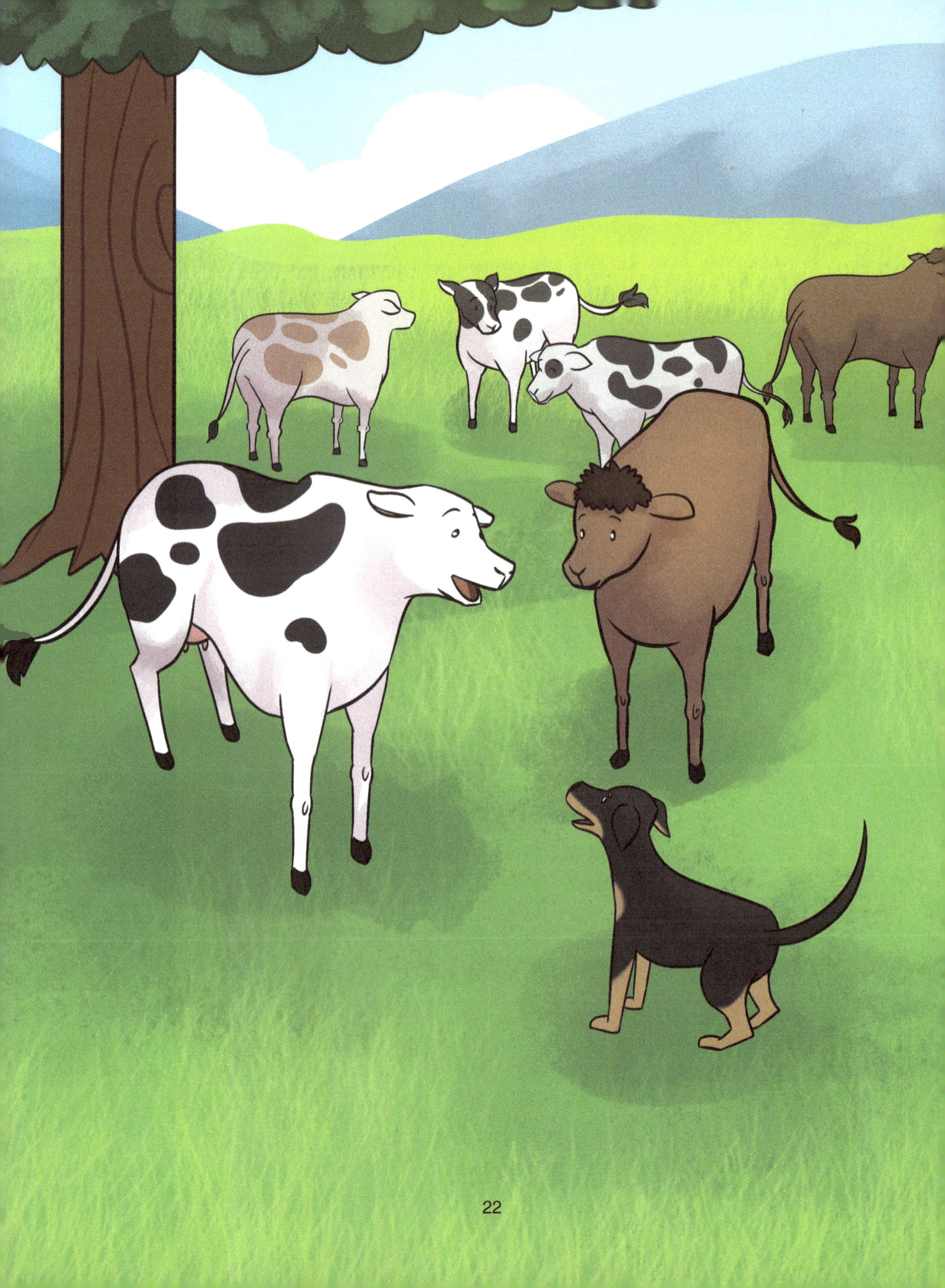

Spark Plug loved herding animals and could do it alone remarkably. He brought a herd of the neighbors' heifers to the barn and other neighbors' goats. Everyone laughed, even the farmers retrieving their animals, loading them into trailers, and taking them home again. Spark Plug sat watching, happy faced and tail spinning fast.

One day, he brought his people a gift, laid it on the front porch, sat beside it after scratching the door, and guarded it until someone responded. Grandmother had a feeling another baby animal awaited her motherly skills. Spark Plug regularly did this. So far, he had brought a baby rabbit, a baby racoon, two baby fawns, and the woodchuck. This was the ultimate gift, a very tiny baby skunk estimated to be a three-day old infant. Proud of his offering, he followed Grandmother in the house, watching every move she made while she was feeding the baby skunk, anxious to wash little stink face off afterward.

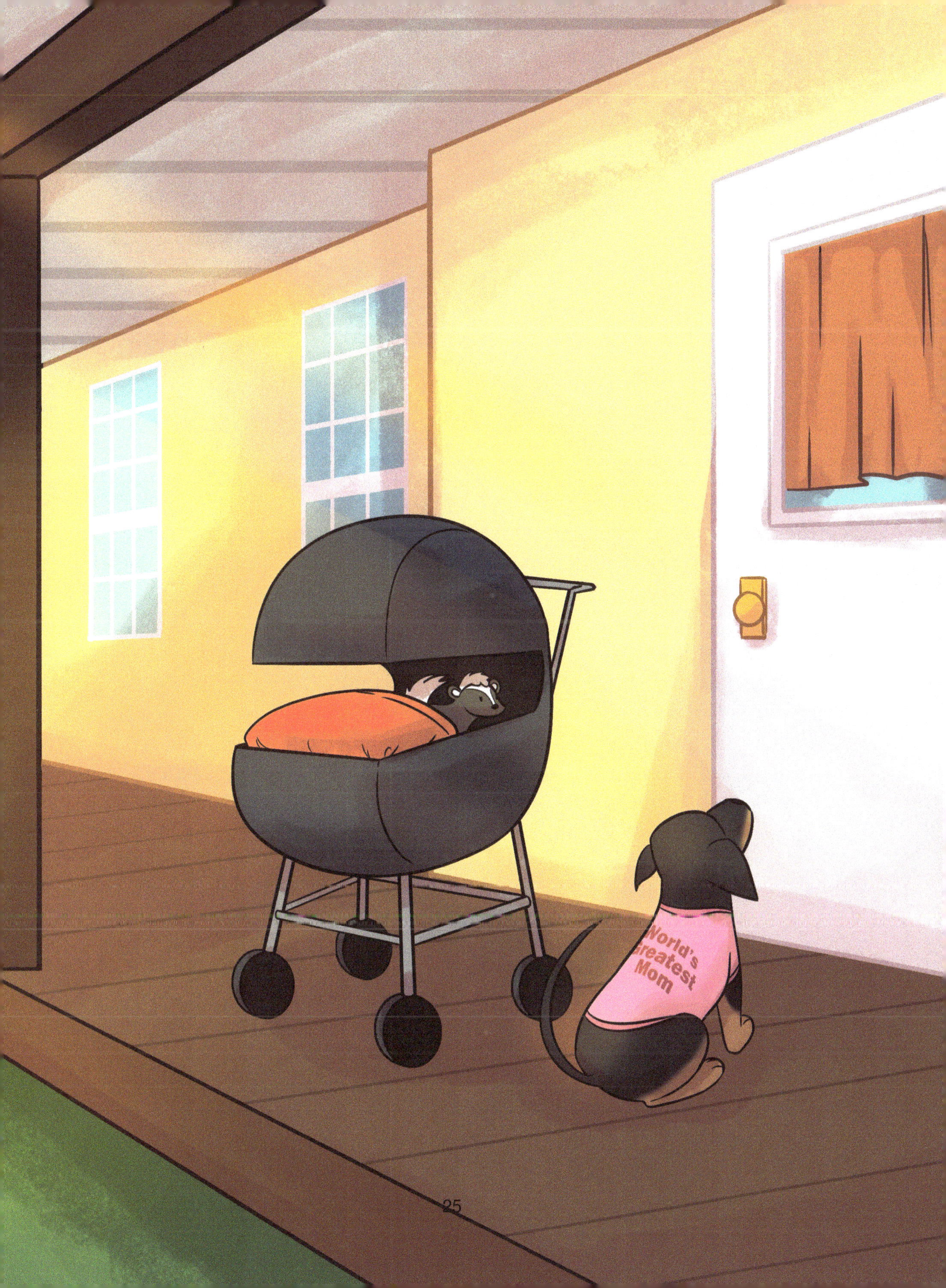
World's
Greatest
Mom

All of Spark Plug's gifts hung around the farm. Occasionally, Spark Plug would play or lick them or just sit quietly watching the landscape together, content with all his animal friends.

Jumping at the front door one day, he was anxious to go outside. It was unusual for the Rottweiler, who normally napped until chore time, to be impatiently asking to go out. Although he had never been sick, she was concerned he was ill and opened the door. He raced out, and Grandmother followed to make sure all was well. Running like a high-speed race car up the dirt road, she saw a large furry animal in the road kicking up dirt and swinging his head back and forth. Spark Plug stopped far from it and stayed there blocking its path, keeping the animal from coming any closer to the farm. Grandfather took the pickup up the road to understand what was happening. Parking by Spark Plug, he could see an enormous rabid ram. White foam around his mouth, it was trying to butt the air. He put Spark Plug in the pickup, lassoed the animal, and tied it to a shade tree. Then he called the game warden to come remove the sick animal, grateful none of his livestock were bitten by the ram and again pleased and grateful for Spark Plug, who was always on alert protecting his farm.

Chapter 4

    One morning, everyone woke to a frantically barking Spark Plug down in the barn. The house was 150 feet from the barn, so to hear the commotion, it needed to be investigated at once. Grandfather grabbed his gun, and off we all went to the barn. It was snowing, so we could not see well, but there were no tracks outside around the doors. Inside, nothing appeared to be missing, but the dog was frantic and wanting to go outside. When we let him out, he flew up the long driveway to the road then back to Grandfather. With years of experience living with Spark Plug, Grandfather knew to trust this dog and went after him. Grandmother and I went to the house. I went to my room and noticed my sister was missing. I searched the house for her, unable to find her anywhere. I told Grandmother, and she insisted she was here somewhere, so we kept looking. It was a fourteen-room two-story farmhouse with an attic, also a woodshed and a walk-in cellar. She could be hiding anywhere. She did sleepwalk, and I found her once on the top shelf of a closet.

While they searched, Grandfather tried to keep up with Spark Plug—no easy task with snow and wind. His tracks were hard to see, and it was still dark. He could hear him and knew he was on his way up past the gully and upper barn and into the dense woods along the logging path.

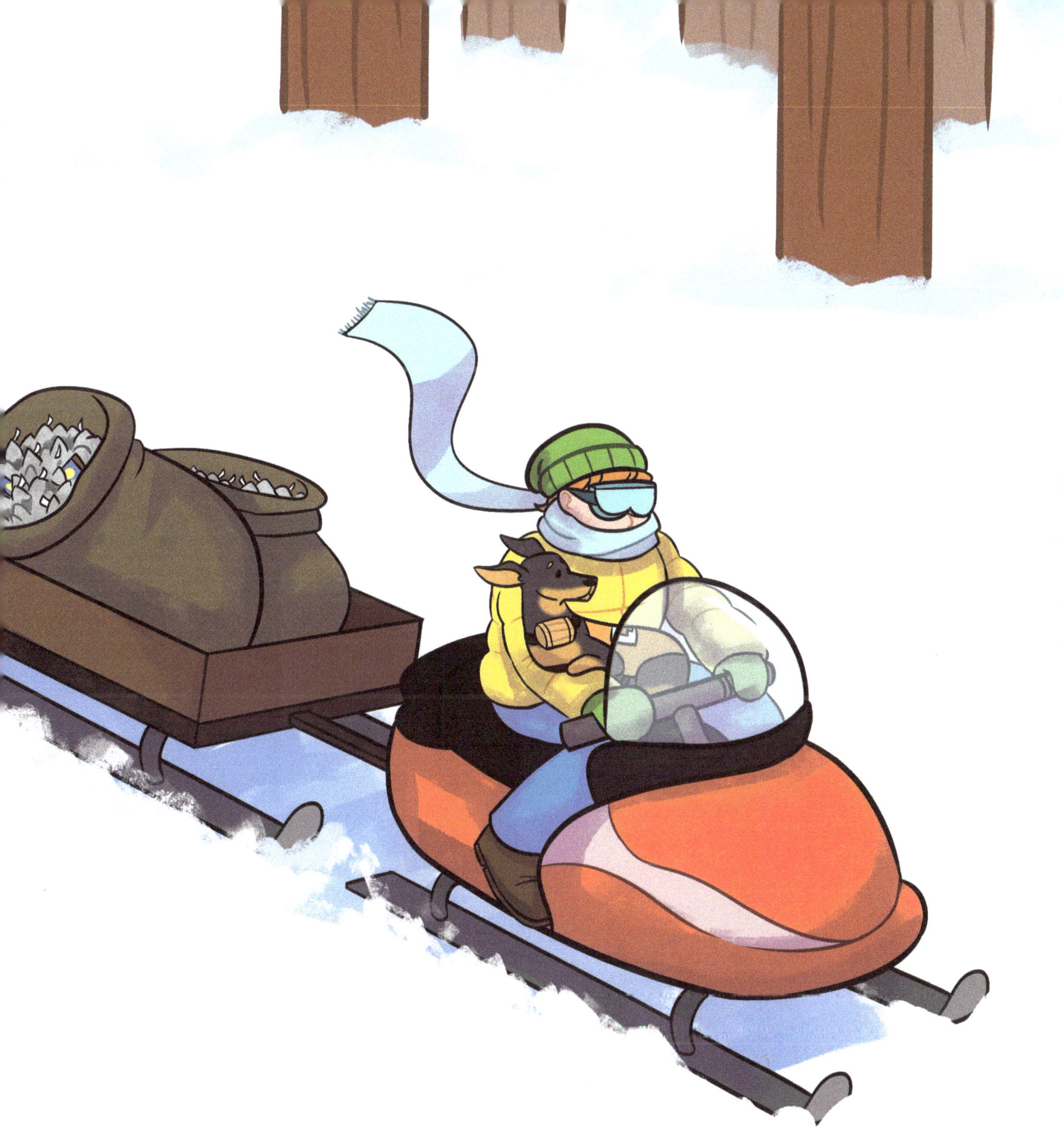

Grandfather guessed a pack of wild dogs passed by and were trying to get in the upper barn, or it was a bear. The snow was falling harder, and the storm was gaining strength. He stopped to listen and was indecisive whether he heard wind or growling, until he heard a faint bark. It sounded like Spark Plug was fighting with an animal as tough and brave as he, and by Spark Plug's barks, Grandfather knew where they were. It was getting lighter. This fight had been going on too long. The barks and growls were weakening. Grandfather was weary too until he heard a child's scream! That infused energy in him, and he ran toward the commotion.

It was Spark Plug in attack mode, head lowered, ears back, legs spread, braced in front of my sister, who was leaning against a fence post, scared and crying. Spark Plug was battling with a wolf, both animals battered and bloody. It was too dark to risk shooting the wolf, so Grandfather shot above them in hopes the wolf, hearing the gun, would retreat. The wolf ran off, and Grandfather checked his granddaughter then Spark Plug, embraced them both, and went home. Lying on his bed with a happy face, Spark Plug lay by the fire. Because of his severe bites needing stitches, the veterinarian came to the farm right away. He looked like a punk rock singer with both sides of his fur shaved off.

32

Later, the townspeople made him a rescue dog coat, and the mayor awarded him a plaque as an official rescue dog of our tiny town population of ninety-eight people. Everyone loved Spark Plug! Spark Plug was not concerned with all the publicity; he just wanted to eat.

Mealtime was his favorite thing. Every day at the same time, no matter what he was doing, his three kittens, now full-grown cats, came to the kitchen, took their places, and waited to be served their own kind of food.

After eating each other's food, the cats would bathe. Spark Plug helped lick their faces too. Occasionally, they had an extra cat join them. Micio, Italian for *cat*, would scratch on the back door and meow. Grandmother would let him in, and he jumped up on the stool by the door. He would not wander through the house; he wanted to eat then go back outside. He was the oldest barn cat we owned. He was around thirty-two years old, and he had lost all his teeth. He brought Grandmother a dead mouse, and she gave him a dish of raw hamburger. It worked out well because the dead mouse would be eaten by Specky, an old female cat who did not hunt any longer. All the animals on the farm lived a long time, and everyone was given a name.

Jumping Jack, one of Spark Plug's kittens, loved answering the telephone. When it rang, he jumped up and knocked the receiver off. When it landed, he would meow into it. He also had an annoying habit of using our toilet instead of his cat box. One day, Grandfather had to use the restroom at the same time as Jumping Jack.

Grandfather brushed him off the toilet, and he jumped into the bathtub and left Grandmother a surprise. We all laughed. Spark Plug never went in the house, even as a baby. He just knew not to do that, which was another amazing thing about him. He knew right from wrong the moment he arrived here—a very clever dog.

Life went on, and we had more adventures together. Spark Plug lived a full life, a happy life. The breeder said Grandfather would not regret taking the dog, and he never did. The breeder stopped by months later, checking up on the dog, and Grandfather thanked him for being insistent on him keeping the puppy, also apologizing and offered to pay the selling cost of this fabulous animal. His worth was so much more than money. The breeder refused the money.

Spark Plug inspired us to live happily every day, day by day. Doing the best with your own unique abilities, spreading kindness and love for all in your hearts, and never being afraid to help those who need it or being cautious of threatening things that come up in life will always keep a spark of joy in your life, and it will always give you a Spark Plug happy face.

The End

Born March of 1960. Spark Plug, six months old

About the Author

Sheri Palmer was born and raised in a tiny town called Birdsall, New York, located in the Allegheny National Forest in Upstate New York, along the Black River.

Sheri graduated from college located in Redding Ridge, Connecticut and began her writing career.

Sheri has many accomplishments, talents, and interests.

You can connect with Sheri on all major social network sites. Sheri is always grateful for her audience and loves reading your comments.

Sheri Palmer hopes everyone enjoys her work and thanks all who read her books.